The SEN Code of Practice in Early Years Settings

by
Dr Hannah Mortimer

A QEd Publication

Published in 2002

© Hannah Mortimer

ISBN 1 898873 28 3

British Library Cataloguing
A catalogue record for this book is available from the British Library.

Published by QEd, The ROM Building, Eastern Avenue,
Lichfield, Staffs. WS13 6RN
Web site: www.qed.uk.com
Email: orders@qed.uk.com

Printed in the United Kingdom by Stowes (Stoke-on-Trent).

Contents

Introduction

Who this book is for

This book will be useful for early years educators working with children with special educational needs (SEN) in all kinds of early years settings: pre-schools, private nurseries, day nurseries and schools. It will also be helpful for individuals training on NVQ or pre-school diploma courses and of interest to childminders, parents and carers of children who have special educational needs in their early years. In other words, it will be of interest to all those who live or work with children who are at the Foundation Stage of their education and have special educational needs.

What the law says

Recent legislation has strengthened the right of parents to have a say in how their children's special educational needs are met and to make sure that children's needs are met inclusively in mainstream settings unless there are good reasons why this should not be the case. Part 4 of the *Education Act 1996* made the revised duties of settings and LEAs clearer and promised a revised *Special Educational Needs Code of Practice* to provide detailed guidance on how these duties could be met. Part 1 of the *SEN and Disability Act* (SENDA, 2001) came into force in January 2002 and amended the 1996 Act to provide more rights for children with statements of SEN to attend mainstream schools. This was followed by a new Code of Practice from the Disability Rights Commission due later in 2002.

The Code of Practice for SEN

The revised *SEN Code of Practice* was issued by the Department for Education and Skills (DfES) in late 2001 and came into force in England in January 2002. Its purpose is to give practical guidance to local education authorities (LEAs), the governing bodies of schools and registered providers of education and to all those who help them including the Health Service and Social Services. All early years settings registered to receive government funding, maintained and non-maintained schools must *have regard to* the Code. This book explains what you have to do.

Most children will have their special educational needs met in the local early years setting. In this book, the term 'settings' is used to describe all early years schools, nurseries and pre-schools, maintained and otherwise, that are registered to receive government funding. We also use the term 'practitioner' to describe all those who work in early years settings: teachers, playleaders and helpers. Some children may require the additional input of LEA support services, or professionals from Health or Social Services. A very small number whose SEN are very complex or severe may need a 'statement of SEN' in which case it is the LEA who decides and arranges how the child's SEN are to be met. The Code also gives clear guidance on how settings should work in partnership with parents and how to involve them in the planning and monitoring of their child's needs.

Providing an inclusive early years curriculum

. Sometimes children will join your setting with their SEN already identified. There may be professionals already involved in supporting the child and they will be able to share information with you to help your planning. However, for other children, their needs might not become clear until they have started to attend an early years setting. The *SEN Code of Practice* gives guidance on when you should start to plan special support and how to do this. How does the practitioner know when to be concerned if a child seems to be developing or behaving differently? What is the legal definition of a 'special educational need'?

Definition of special educational needs

The definition of SEN is widely understood as being about children and young people with learning difficulties. It is important to recognise that the definition of children with learning difficulties *includes* children with a disability where any special educational provision needs to be made. This does not mean that children with a disability necessarily have learning difficulties, or that only disabled children with learning difficulties have special educational needs. It does mean that children with a disability have special educational needs *if they have any difficulty in accessing education* and if they need any special educational provision to be made for them.

In any early years setting there are likely to be children at very different stages of development. Each child is a unique individual who brings his or her own experiences and particular pattern of developing and behaving to any learning situation. In time, it might become clear to those working with a child that there are special educational needs. How does the practitioner know when to be concerned if a child seems to be developing differently? What is the legal definition of a 'special educational need'?

Definition of Special Educational Needs

A child has special educational needs if he or she has a *learning difficulty* which calls for *special educational provision* to be made for him or her.

A child has a *learning difficulty* if he or she:

(a) has a significantly greater difficulty in learning than the majority of children of the same age; or
(b) has a disability that prevents or hinders them from making use of educational facilities of a kind generally provided for children of the same age in schools within the area of the local education authority;
(c) is under five and falls within the definition at (a) or (b) above or would do if special educational provision were not made for the child.

A child must not be regarded as having a learning difficulty solely because the language or medium of communication of the home is different from the language in which he or she is or will be taught.

Special educational provision means:

(a) for a child over two, educational provision which is additional to, or otherwise different from, the educational provision made generally for children of the child's age in maintained schools, other than special schools, in the area;
(b) for a child under two, educational provision of any kind.

(from *Education Act 1996*, Section 312)

The *Education Act 1996* tells us that any difficulty must be *significant*, over and above what you would expect from the child's age, and affect the child's ability to access the play and learning activities which your setting provides. It is not sufficient for the child to be different. So to speak a language different from the majority of the group, or to suffer a medical condition which does not affect day-to-day learning, will not represent a 'special educational need'.

Children might be described as having SEN for many different reasons; for example, a child with a physical disability who has difficulty accessing education; or a child with developmental delay; or a child with a language and communication difficulty; or a child with behaviour or emotional difficulties. You might find the Scholastic series *Special Needs in the Early Years* helpful if you are working with children with particular areas of need or disabilities. Early years practitioners now have a duty to recognise and identify any special educational needs within their setting so that they can plan what action they can take to support and help the child.

The fundamental principles underlying the *SEN Code of Practice* are that:
- children with SEN should have their needs met;

- this should normally be in the mainstream setting;

- children's views should be sought and taken into account;

- parents play a vital role as well;

- early years children with SEN should be offered a broad, balanced and relevant Foundation Stage curriculum.

How to use this book

In Chapter One, you will learn how to design an inclusive SEN policy for your early years setting. All settings should now have such a policy and you should review its effectiveness and inclusiveness regularly. Chapter Two describes the role of the SEN Co-ordinator. Each registered early years setting should have a member of staff appointed with special responsibility for SEN.

Chapter Three shows how you can set up SEN procedures and describes how you can plan inclusive and differentiated provision. In Chapter Four you will be helped to design and implement Individual Education Plans (IEPs). Chapter Five shows how you can monitor SEN provision and describes a graduated approach to planning and monitoring.

Chapter Six indicates how you can work in partnership with parents and children, and Chapter Seven provides pointers for working in partnership with others. Chapter Eight discusses ways in which you can make sure that the children themselves are involved in the way you plan for and meet their needs. There is a section on useful books and references at the end of the book. Readers who wish to look at the subject in greater depth might find the book *Special Needs and Early Years Provision* (Mortimer, 2001) helpful.

Chapter One

The SEN Policy

What is the SEN policy?

All registered early years settings should have an SEN policy in place (see page 44 for an example). Your policy should contain the following information:

A summary

It should begin with a short summary of the beliefs shared by staff regarding children who have SEN. You might, for example, say that you want all children to be entitled to a broad, balanced and purposeful early years curriculum and that you will work with parents and other agencies to achieve this.

How will you achieve this entitlement?

The policy should then say how you will do this. How will you decide which children need help and what will you do about it? How will you monitor, record and evaluate all children's progress and identify, assess and review any special needs? How will you provide additional resources and support for children with SEN? How will you publish admissions arrangements in relation to children who have SEN and how will you consider complaints about SEN provision within the setting?

Who is responsible?

Finally, your policy should provide information on the name of the setting's member of staff with responsibility for the day-to-day operation of the SEN policy, any SEN expertise and qualifications of the staff within the setting, and how you will all obtain training on SEN. What resources for supporting SEN are already available within the setting, who are your local support services, and how do you access them if you need to?

Developing an inclusive policy

What should an inclusive SEN policy look like? It should make it clear that the setting welcomes all children whatever their individual needs. This should be clearly stated in any parents' handbooks. To make this possible, the curriculum planning should be suitable for all children with opportunities for all children to have positive outcomes from each learning opportunity. Staff members should have opportunities to take up training in both SEN and Early Years (EY) practice and *everyone* should share a responsibility for meeting the requirements of the *SEN Code of Practice*. Observations and planning should be shared regularly with parents. Those involved should all be flexible enough to change what is being done in order to meet a particular child's needs. Methods of communication should include everyone and could also be used between children. There should be a willingness to involve professionals from outside agencies and to include them in SEN planning. All staff should work and plan together to meet any special educational needs and you should be able to provide families with the names and contact details of the relevant support services that might help them.

Regular review

Your setting's SEN policy needs to be brought up to date whenever there is new legislation. This means that it will have been updated following the new *SEN Code of Practice* in 2001 and the *Disability Rights Commission Code of Practice* in late 2002. It should also be reviewed annually anyway, involving colleagues in discussions about how effective it has been and how well it is supporting children who have SEN. The day-to-day operation of the SEN policy is the role of the setting's special educational needs co-ordinator or 'SENCO'. In the next chapter, we discuss the role and responsibilities of this person.

Chapter Two

The SEN Co-ordinator

Why appoint a SENCO?

The *SEN Code of Practice* states that each registered early years setting should have a member of staff appointed with special responsibility for SEN. The usual term for this person is a 'special educational needs co-ordinator' or 'SENCO'. This person will have responsibility for the day-to-day operation of the SEN policy, developing SEN expertise and qualifications of the staff within the setting, developing partnership with parents and carers concerning SEN, and helping staff obtain training on SEN. This person will also monitor what resources are available for supporting SEN within the setting, who the local support services are, and how they can be accessed if required. All of this will take time, and the Code suggests that the management group or headteacher think carefully about giving the SENCO protected time for these duties.

There are plans for all early years SENCOs to receive training over the next few years. There are also plans for 850 area SENCOs by 2004, each providing support for about 20 early years settings. There will be local variations on how this is achieved and several pilot SENCO support schemes are already being set up. This means that it is an exciting time for developing SEN training and support in early years.

What the SENCO does

The Code describes four main responsibilities for SENCOs. They should:

- make sure that there is liaison with parents and other professionals when assessing, planning for and supporting children who have SEN;

- advise and support other practitioners in the setting;

- make sure that appropriate IEPs are in place for each child who has SEN (see Chapter Four);

- make sure that relevant background information about individual children is collected, recorded and kept up to date.

In early years settings, SENCOs might be chosen because of their special interest in SEN, because they have worked previously with children who have SEN, or because they already have some SEN training. Sometimes it is a promoted post and the postholder also has input to the senior management team of a school or nursery. It is important that the SENCO has a genuine interest and commitment to meeting children's SEN in the early years and to doing so inclusively and through equal opportunity.

Identifying and assessing SEN

The SENCO should take the lead in assessing a child's strengths and weaknesses when it is felt that the child might have SEN. You will find the book *The Observation and Assessment of Children in the Early Years* (Mortimer, 2001) a useful tool. Many practitioners now use the framework *Curriculum Guidance for the Foundation Stage* (QCA, 2001) to help them do this, identifying stepping stones or achievements which the child has reached in each area of learning, and pointing out Early Learning Goals or stepping stones still to be achieved.

Careful and accurate observation and assessment will provide a record of the progress that each child makes. Of course, not all children will make the same rate of progress and it is necessary for the SENCO or practitioner to use their judgement about what they might reasonably expect to be 'adequate' progress. A key test for action, then, would be if the progress a child was making was felt to be inadequate based on what could be reasonably expected. The Code states that when a practitioner who works day-to-day with a child, or the SENCO, identifies a child who is making inadequate progress, i.e. has special educational needs, they should plan interventions which are *additional to* or *different from* those provided by the setting's usual range of strategies or curriculum. How this might be done will be dealt with in the next chapter. The SENCO must therefore work closely with colleagues to plan effective strategies and to monitor how these are making a difference for the child. This will involve careful record keeping.

As well as the usual pupil records kept by the setting, the pupil record or profile for a child with SEN should contain information about the child's progress from the setting, from parents and from other services and professionals. These records are usually kept by the SENCO. The records should also include the child's own perceptions and views of their difficulties and their progress as far as they are able to contribute. This might be through photographic records of the child's enjoyment and successes, through records of things they have said, and through examples of their work and creations. The booklet *Taking Part* (Mortimer, 2000) is particularly helpful in doing this as it collects the child's own views during the process of assessment.

Planning 'Early Years Action'

When a practitioner or SENCO identifies a child with SEN and plans interventions which are *additional to* or *different from* those provided by the setting's usual range of strategies or curriculum, this is known as taking 'Early Years Action'. What are the roles and responsibilities of the SENCO during Early Years Action?

It is the SENCO who discusses a child's needs with the practitioner involved with the child and agrees that Early Years Action will be taken. The SENCO makes an informal assessment and gathers information about the child, building up a file, or ring binder, of useful observations, records, assessments and plans. The SENCO makes sure that parents know that the setting is planning additional and different provision to help their child and makes sure they are fully consulted and kept in touch. The SENCO draws up an individual education plan to help the child make progress (Chapter Four). The SENCO arranges regular reviews (usually termly) with parents or carers and the practitioner(s) involved in order to review the IEP and set the next. The SENCO also helps to decide when the child no longer needs special educational provision (the 'additional and different') or when support and advice of outside professionals is needed ('Early Years Action Plus').

Taking 'Early Years Action Plus'

Hopefully, any decision to take Early Years Action Plus will arise naturally out of a regular review meeting to discuss the progress and needs of the child. It is the SENCO's responsibility to make sure that parents and carers know that Early Years Action Plus is to be started. The SENCO completes the necessary paperwork in order to request a referral from the support services – information about your particular procedures can be obtained through your LEA support services or Early Years Childcare and Development Partnership (EYCDP). The SENCO then works closely with the outside professional or agency to provide support for the child with SEN. The SENCO continues to draw up IEPs in co-operation with the outside professional and to organise and co-ordinate the review meetings.

Requests for statutory assessment

If it becomes clear that a child's SEN are significant and his/her needs cannot be met effectively with the resources normally available to the setting, then the SENCO also plays a role in requesting the LEA to consider a statutory assessment of the child's SEN. This is the formal process which can lead to a child receiving a 'statement' of SEN – a kind of prescription detailing what the child's SEN are and how they will be met. It then becomes the responsibility of the LEA to make sure that the needs are met. If a statutory assessment is being requested, the SENCO has to collect all previous information about the child's SEN (IEPs, review meeting notes, previous reports) and send it to the LEA with the necessary paperwork. The SENCO continues to monitor and review the child's progress with the practitioner(s) involved, the parents and carers and the outside professional(s).

In the next chapter, we look at how the SENCO might work with colleagues, managers or governors to design effective and inclusive SEN procedures.

Chapter Three

Setting up SEN procedures

The *SEN Code of Practice* recommends that settings should provide a graduated response to children with SEN. At first, you need procedures for *identifying* children with SEN. Then you need procedures for planning *interventions* that are additional to and different from your usual range of approaches. You should *monitor* and *review* these interventions so that you can all see whether the child is making reasonable progress. If 'more' seems to be needed, you gradually step up your interventions and bring on board outside professionals if necessary. The interventions which you plan and monitor within the setting are called taking Early Years Action. When you are also working alongside outside professionals, this is called 'Early Years Action Plus'. For just a few children (about 1% to 2% of all children up to 18), the SEN will be so great that the setting or parents might consider initiating a 'statutory assessment'. This involves the Local Education Authority (LEA) and may lead to a 'statement of SEN'.

Procedures for identifying SEN

Try not to be daunted by the *SEN Code of Practice*. The best procedures for identifying SEN will arise out of your own regular assessment and monitoring approaches which you use for all the children. The key trigger for action will be when your regular assessment shows 'inadequate progress'. Children with SEN do not require an outside professional to diagnose and proclaim upon them. Instead, try to see *yourselves* as having an expertise in how children learn in the early years. You are therefore in a good position to know when something 'additional' or 'different' is needed in order to help a child make progress. The key to meeting SEN successfully will be your existing flexibility and range of provision. The very fact that you are an early years setting means that you are well used to meeting needs flexibly and catering for a wide range of children's maturity and needs.

When you are planning how to deliver the Foundation Stage curriculum to all your children, you will have allowed for opportunities to assess and observe how each individual child is responding and making progress. From this information, it may become clear to you that, even after a reasonable settling in period, a child is failing to make progress in one or more Areas of Learning – personal, social and emotional development, language and literacy, mathematical development, knowledge and understanding of the world, physical development or creative development. Armed with this knowledge, you can plan what you need to do which is additional to or different from your usual approaches and record this on an individual education plan (see next chapter).

Try to be pragmatic and flexible about this – if it comes to the point that you need to plan 'additional' and 'different' approaches, then this is the stage when you are taking steps to meet SEN. Parents must be told and you need to share your approaches. For many children, your interventions will actually work and that child will no longer need SEN provision, so you need *not* feel that you are somehow 'labelling' a child for evermore. You will find the book from this series *The Observation and Assessment of Children in the Early Years* (Mortimer, 2001) a helpful tool in identifying and assessing children with SEN.

Sometimes you will already know that a child has SEN when that child joins your setting. There should be records available from a previous setting or from professionals who have been involved in the past which should help you plan your 'additional' and 'different' approaches. We are required to meet SEN as inclusively as possible and it will be helpful to think for a moment about what inclusive practice might look like.

What factors support inclusive practices?

Sebba and Sachdev (1997) suggest that these practices support inclusion:

- careful joint planning, especially to make sure that any within-class support is used effectively;

- the use of educational labels rather than categories or medical labels (such as 'co-ordination difficulty' rather than 'dyspraxia', or even 'child who has SEN' rather than 'SEN child');

- teachers and adults who provide good role models for the children because of their positive expectations and the way they respect and value the children;

- the use of strategies that improve children's communication skills;

- the use of teaching strategies that enable all children to participate and learn;

- individual approaches which draw on pupils' earlier experiences, set high expectations, and encourage mutual peer support;

- the flexible use of support aimed to promote joining in and inclusion rather than to create barriers and exclusion.

Providing differentiated approaches

When you are planning interventions for a child with SEN it is helpful to think about how you might make the Foundation Stage curriculum more accessible for a child who is learning or behaving differently from the rest. The process of making activities more accessible and successful for a child with SEN is called 'differentiation'. You can do this in many ways. The National Early Years Network has produced a practical handbook for early years practitioners on how to create inclusive services for disabled children and their families (Dickins and Denziloe, 1998). The authors encourage making play and learning approaches accessible for *all* children wherever possible. You do not have to have 'special' activities for 'special' children or buy plenty of 'special needs' equipment. So often, an activity can be changed in some way. You should never exclude certain children from it because they cannot 'fit in' with it. Flexible approaches and adaptable timetables and routines make this easier.

For example, indoor tables and equipment need to be at adjustable heights and floor spaces comfortable and safe to play on. Acoustics can be softened with soft surfaces, cushions, carpets and curtains, making it easier for everyone to hear clearly. Story times can be kept concrete by using props and visual aids. Outdoor play areas need to contain quiet, sheltered spaces as well as busy active areas. Communication between everybody can be made possible by making sure that all adults are familiar with any language or communication system used by the children. Children can also have a communication book showing how they make their needs and feelings known. You can also make much more use of colours, textures and smells to encourage different senses.

Building on strengths

A good starting point for differentiation is to look at a child's particular strengths and interests. It is important to build on children's strengths if they are to cope with the content of what is on offer more successfully. Choose stories, for example, that are about something the child enjoys and are at a level appropriate to the child's stage of language. Include concrete props to hold attention, emphasise meaning and allow a child to participate with more than one sense at once.

Some children take longer to respond to directions and ideas than others. You might need to allow the child extra time to respond, or allow them to 'get there first' to build up confidence. Activities may be presented at a slower pace to ensure understanding or a succession of materials presented to maintain interest during a discussion. Some children need to 'sandwich' short periods of structured activity with periods of free play or quiet. Sometimes children find it hard to remember more than the last piece of information given them and therefore need supporting and prompting at each step, taking longer to carry out structured activities.

All planning for the Early Learning Goals will include a degree of planning for different levels of children's ability. Within this, it might be that some children need the learning steps broken down further, and it may be necessary to give value to a smaller and less obvious learning outcome or 'stepping stone'. You might also need to present the activities in a different way. Some children may need adapted scissors to cut out a picture, or require photographs rather than line drawings in order to name objects. Some might need toys and playthings that are easy to handle (such as form-boards with knobs on the pieces). Others might need tabletops at a suitable height for them to access when in a standing frame. Some might need radio hearing aids to hear, or to sit close up to large picture books to see.

Think about how you will encourage the child to communicate with you and with the other children. Some rely on sign language to make their sounds clear. Others may not be able to tell you their wishes, but can demonstrate by their smiles or their choices where they would like to play. If attention is short, it might be necessary to revisit an activity at another time in order to ensure success. Some children find it harder to settle and to concentrate after they have been very active. Others need to 'let off steam' for a while in order to return more attentively to an activity.

Structure and grouping

Some children respond best in a highly structured setting, led and supported by a practitioner or helper. Others seem to respond best in free play. Every child needs opportunities to play and to learn both on their own terms and in groups with other adults and children. Some children need more individual adult support and time. This can include some one-to-one work or withdrawal into a small group, but mainly refers to supporting the child with additional encouragement and prompting within the regular group. In an inclusive setting, any time spent relating individually to an adult would take place in the nursery room itself, with opportunities for involving other children as well.

Working in groups provides good models for the child with SEN. Sometimes meeting the needs of individual children with SEN has led to children working alone on individual materials. Arrangements to include the child's IEP within planning for the whole group can overcome this and lead to a more purposeful and supportive way of meeting SEN. It is also possible for you to plan interventions through a 'Group IEP', especially when there are several children with similar needs. In the next chapter, we look at how you can design and write an individual education plan for a child with SEN. This will give you a tool with which you can monitor and review progress with colleagues and parents or carers.

Chapter Four

Designing and implementing
Individual Education Plans

As well as a revised *SEN Code of Practice*, the DfES has produced a 'Toolkit' for helping practitioners understand the requirements of the Code (see page 50). Section 5 of this Toolkit deals with managing individual education plans or IEPs. An IEP is simply a planning, teaching and reviewing tool. It does not contain everything you wish the child with SEN to learn. It picks out three or four targets against which future progress can be measured. The IEP should underpin all your planning and intervention for the child with SEN and should, therefore, be shared with colleagues, parents and carers.

The IEP must contain certain basic information:

• *what* should be taught;

• *how* it should be taught;

• *how often* the additional or different provision will be made.

There is no set format. You need to design an IEP that is clear, accessible and understandable. All children with SEN (whether you are taking Early Years Action, Early Years Action Plus or whether the child has a statement) should have an IEP in place which is reviewed regularly – usually once a term in the early years.

What information should you include?

Depending on the child's particular difficulties, you will be choosing three or four key targets to be met in the short term. Most IEPs start by stating what the child's difficulties are and many also state the child's strengths and particular interests. The IEP then details:

• the short-term targets set for the child;

21

- the teaching approaches to be used;

- what you will do that is additional or different;

- how often this will be carried out;

- when you will review the plan;

- how you will know whether you have been successful;

- what outcomes you will observe or measure.

The whole idea is that IEPs should result in a child making progress. They therefore need to be manageable, easily understandable by others, jargon free and dovetail with your Foundation Stage curriculum for all the children. The suggestion is that the targets should be 'SMART' – specific, measurable, achievable, relevant and time-bound. You need to write them in terms of what the child will do (rather than what you will do), so they always start with the child's name. There is a booklet published by the Pre-school Learning Alliance, *The Role of the Special Educational Needs Co-ordinator (SENCO) in Pre-school Settings*, which suggests different formats for your IEP (see page 51). Here is one possible example.

Individual Education Plan

Name: Josie Bates   **Early Years Action**

Nature of Difficulty

Josie finds it hard to sit still and to concentrate. Sometimes her play is over-boisterous and other children can get hurt.

Strengths

Josie loves physical play. She also enjoys music time. She is friendly and wants to please people.

Action   Who will do what?

1. Sam, Josie's keyworker, will play alongside Josie and two or three other children and help her to play gently.

2. We will use Music Time to encourage Josie to look and listen and to join in for longer periods of time.

3. We will start with story time in a quiet area with one adult and then gradually include more children in the group.

4. We will all use Josie's name and engage eye contact with her before we speak to her.

5. We will always show her what to do as well as tell her.

Help from parents

1. Mrs Bates will use the same approaches when talking to Josie.

2. She will spend five minutes each night on a bedtime story.

Targets for this term

Personal, social and emotional development

Josie will play with an adult and another child for ten minutes without becoming boisterous.

Language, literacy and communication

1. Josie will look at an adult briefly when they are talking to her.

2. Josie will settle in the book corner with an adult for five minutes looking at a picture book.

Creative development

Josie will join in at Music Time for a full 20 minutes.

Any pastoral or medical requirements

Josie is being referred by her GP to the Community Paediatrician because of her level of activity and poor attention.

Monitoring and assessment arrangements

Sam will observe Josie each month. We will all keep a record of particularly challenging or successful times, noting what happened, what led up to it and what happened next as a result.

Review meeting with parents

Next term (plus date)

Other people to invite

Perhaps the health visitor could let us know what happened with the paediatrician?

Once you have an IEP in place and it is shared by all the staff, it becomes possible to monitor a child's progress in light of the targets you have set. A simple monitoring sheet can be used which might look something like this.

Date	Activity	Observations	Staff

In the next chapter, we look in more detail at how SENCOs can monitor the graduated SEN provision which is being made.

Chapter Five

Monitoring SEN provision

A graduated approach

We have seen how there are different 'grades' of response to meeting a child's SEN, depending on how great the child's difficulties are. We have also seen how one type of response does not necessarily lead to more and more help, since the idea is that you will actually help children overcome some of their difficulties through the interventions you provide. It will be helpful to summarise this graduated approach.

Approach	Response to SEN	Whose responsibility?
Identification	Practitioner notices that a child is failing to make progress, even after a settling in period.	Setting
Early Years Action	Parents are informed. SENCO and colleagues gather information. SENCO draws up IEP and plans interventions which practitioners carry out with SENCO's help. IEPs are reviewed with parents or carers.	Setting
Early Years Action Plus	SENCO brings in outside specialists to advise further. IEPs continue based on this advice.	Setting
Statutory assessment	LEA considers need for a statutory assessment and calls for reports. IEPs continue.	Setting and LEA
Statement	LEA considers if a statement is needed. If so, it monitors and reviews the SEN provision.	Setting and LEA

Monitoring provision

The SENCO needs to keep tabs on what SEN provision is being made and how the child is making progress. Some find it useful to keep a ring folder into which they will file:

- when and why they were first concerned;

- their assessments and observations;

- records of their contact with parents and carers;

- IEPs;

- notes from IEP review meetings;

- copy of any referral to outside professionals;

- correspondence from professionals or the LEA;

- copies of reports received.

This should be a working file and it should be transparent how information received or gathered about the child has led to clear plans, interventions and reviews. In other words, you have followed an 'assess – plan – intervene – review' cycle. *How to Survive and Succeed as a SENCO in the Primary School* (Birkett, 2000) provides some helpful suggestions about proformas for various records that the SENCO in a primary school (including Foundation Stage) might wish to keep.

If it seems clear that a child is not making sufficient progress despite the interventions you have planned through Early Years Action and Early Years Action Plus, then you might be requesting the LEA to consider initiating a statutory assessment of the child's SEN. By this stage, there will be an outside professional involved who can advise you. There are strict time limits within which the LEA must make decisions about this. The LEA will probably contact all those involved, including the parents and carers, to gather information and decide on the level of the child's needs. Parents themselves can request such an assessment and can be supported by an Independent Parental Supporter to help them through the SEN process. The LEA SEN Section can tell you how to contact these people.

If the LEA decides to initiate a statutory assessment, formal reports will be requested from the school doctor or paediatrician, the educational psychologist, a teacher and Social Services (if involved). Parents or carers and the child (see Chapter Eight) will also be asked to contribute. The 'evidence' will be collected together and, if it is warranted, a statement will be drawn up by the LEA. This will state what the child's needs are and what SEN provision will be made. Parents will be asked to suggest the school or setting where they would like their child's needs to be met. Again, this whole process has a strict time limit and should take no longer than six months to complete. Once the child has a statement of SEN, the LEA itself monitors the provision. There will be regular reviews (six-monthly in the Foundation Stage) to make sure that the statement is still needed and that it is up to date.

Keeping records

The SENCO might find it useful to set up an easy record-keeping system for keeping tabs on what SEN provision is being made for a child and how it is being reviewed. It might look something like this.

Early Years Action						
Name	Date of birth	Parents/ carers informed	Initial meeting date	First review date	Second review date	Outcome

Early Years Action Plus						
Name	Date of birth	Outside agency involved	Initial meeting date	First review date	Second review date	Outcome

Children with statements				
Name	Date of birth	Date of statement	Provision specified	Date of review

Chapter Six

Working in partnership with parents

Parental rights

Recent legislation has strengthened the rights of parents when their child has SEN. Parents can now expect the setting to provide the name of the SENCO, explain its arrangements for deciding which children need help and how this will be given (this should be part of the SEN policy), and describe how it will work with parents. Parents must be informed if SEN provision is felt to be needed for their child – i.e. the stage at which you decide to plan Early Years Action. The whole SEN process has to be transparent and shared. This poses new challenges for early years practitioners and in this chapter we look at ways of meeting these.

Children's first educators are their parents or carers and we should support them in supporting their children. There are various community SURE START and parenting education programmes which help parents and carers to encourage their children's early learning and development, help them have realistic expectations, help them manage behaviour and support them in becoming more confident parents. Consider how your setting might play a role in parent education. Look for ways of involving parents and carers in their children's learning, share the reasoning behind your activities and encourage a two-way partnership between home and setting.

Parent partnership

The involvement of parents at all stages is a basic principle of the *SEN Code of Practice*. What approaches seem to be effective for developing a real partnership between parents and early years practitioners?

- You need to respect the fundamental role that parents have already played in their child's education – much will have been learned before the child ever joined your setting.

- Look for ways of sharing learning between home and setting. This is done through mutual respect, ongoing communication and regular information. How can you support what parents are hoping to achieve for their children? How can parents support you in what you are trying to teach in the setting?

- Make sure that parents and carers feel welcome in your setting and that there are opportunities for keeping in touch regularly, personally or by using a home-setting diary.

- Share good news and information at all stages of the children's learning and progress (and not just when there is a problem).

- Check that your admission procedures are flexible, allow time for discussion with parents and for children to feel secure when they first join your setting.

When any child first starts in a new setting, it is a sensitive time for all parents. For a parent of a child known to have SEN, there are even more concerns and mixed emotions wrapped up in the business of sending the child to a new setting. You can understand that sensitive handling will be vital for effective partnership. If possible, spend time before a child joins your setting gathering information and establishing a relationship with child and parents. A home visit is usually helpful, sharing photographs of your group and talking about your typical sessions. Asking positive, open-ended questions can provide information about the child's strengths and about the kind of help that they need. You will find practical examples of how you can develop your partnership with parents in the series handbook *Meeting SEN in Early Years* published by Scholastic (page 51).

Play plans

One useful way of developing a practical partnership with parents of a child with SEN is to negotiate a 'play plan' to share with parents. This contains ideas for supporting their child's learning at home. The play plan can link in with the child's Individual Education Plan (page 23). This example is a play plan for Josie, the little girl with attention difficulties who we met on page 23. The first sheet is shared with parents who take it home and try out the ideas. The second sheet has parents' comments on how well Josie managed the task, which they bring back to share with the setting.

Play Plan for Josie

Play helps Josie to look, listen and play appropriately with her friends.

Getting started

Say Josie's name when you want to talk to her and make eye contact with her. Give lots of praise and show her how pleased you are when she looks and listens.

Games to play

1. Table games: use 'Picture lotto' or 'SNAP' games to hold her attention and help her to take turns.

2. Give Josie a sticker every time she plays well with another child. Play beside her to help it go smoothly and praise her for being gentle.

3. Spend five minutes each night with a bedtime story to build up her attention and concentration.

How to help

As Josie becomes more able to attend, build up the story and play times so she manages for longer.

How did Josie get on?

Monday

She hates it when I try to get her eye contact but I'll stick at it.

Tuesday

Today Josie looks at me just for a moment when I speak – it's probably to get me off her back!

Thursday

We had a bad time when Charlie came to play, but I think it was because I wasn't with her. She rugby tackled her to the floor more than once! Yet she gets really upset when Charlie cries.

Making home-setting links

Early years settings have developed many different ways of developing their links with parents. Here are some examples:

- The setting up of a toy and resource library in the setting for children and parents or carers to borrow from.

- Foundation Stage curriculum workshops for parents and educators to share.

- A bookshelf with useful pamphlets for parents and carers on many topics including SEN, Lifelong Learning, local libraries and community resources.

- An 'open door' policy for parents or carers to call in to talk with approachable staff at mutually convenient times.

- Multicultural story and craft sessions by parents and extended family members.

- 'Borrowing' specialist skills from parents or members of the community to share with the children – musicians, artists, industrialists, actors, cooks, footballers, craftworkers.

- A refreshment and social room/corner for parents and younger family members.

- Within-setting parenting groups to address areas of concern, such as children's behaviour.

- Discussion groups for talking about areas of common interest (such as story sacks or getting ready for school) in order to share ideas and strategies.

- Regular parent education programmes tailor-made to the needs of the community and the cultures.

- Regular use of monitoring questionnaires and feedback forms.

- Multilingual parents' notice boards and newsletters.

- Music-maker groups to welcome in parents and younger children with SEN in the locality (you might find the 'Music Makers' material helpful; see page 50).

- Action research within the setting designed by both professionals and parents.

In the next chapter, we look at the other professionals you might work with when you are assessing and working with a child who has SEN.

Chapter Seven

Working in partnership with others

Outside professionals

In this chapter, we meet the outside professionals who might be advising and supporting you and the child who has SEN through Early Years Action Plus or through the child's statement of SEN. Usually, these professionals will work for the LEA or the Health Service. Sometimes you might be working alongside colleagues from Social Services or a professional from a voluntary organisation such as MENCAP or Barnardos.

The LEA

Each LEA has its own way of organising its support services and you will need to find out who the professionals are in your area and how you access them when you are putting together your SEN Policy. Some LEAs have general support services available to children from the early years through to age 19. More and more are developing early years support services in conjunction with the Early Years Childcare and Development Partnership. If that is the case for you, there is probably a named early years support teacher and educational psychologist for your area. Sometimes they work in a consultative way, discussing the child's difficulties and needs with you and the carers and helping you develop strategies for supporting the child. Sometimes, they will arrange to see the child to add to your assessment and information gathering and to suggest ways forward. If your setting is registered with the Partnership, all this kind of information should be available to you already.

Early years support teachers are well placed to advise you on a child's strengths and difficulties within the Foundation Stage curriculum. They can advise you on how to assess these and make suggestions for IEPs and strategies to help the child make progress. They also have a working knowledge of the SEN procedures so can help to guide you through your monitoring and reviewing. They will know about local schools and resources and can be especially helpful in helping you prepare a child for starting school and make the transfer go as smoothly as possible for child and family. Sometimes they have particular knowledge or expertise in helping children with a particular area of need, such as autism or behaviour difficulty.

In some areas it is the **educational psychologist** whom you would meet first. Educational psychologists are teachers who have gone on to specialise in how children develop, behave and learn. They work with settings and parents or carers to assess children's needs and to see if, together, you can all make a difference to the child's progress. Generally, they would visit the child in the setting and also meet with parents and carers. They have a particular knowledge of child development and of particular disabilities and learning difficulties. If a child's needs are felt to be great enough to warrant statutory assessment, then the educational psychologist has to provide a formal report to go with this. Usually, you will find that the educational psychologist works with you to assess a child's needs in the setting over a period of time so that the educational psychology assessment is not static, 'one-off' and carried out in a strange situation.

Some LEAs, multidisciplinary groups or voluntary organisations also run a **Portage service**. Portage is a home-visiting service in which parents or carers are supported in encouraging their child's development step by small step. You may meet a Portage home visitor or a Portage supervisor when a child first joins you. Quite often, Portage services stop once a child is in an early years setting, though you will probably be able to make use of the checklist that has been used and build on the teaching that was effective for that child.

The Health Service

All children should have access to a health visitor and this person can be a useful source of information when a child first joins you, particularly if there is a medical condition, developmental delay, family difficulty or sensory loss (hearing or vision). If there have been concerns at developmental checks, then it is likely that a child will also be known to a child health clinic **doctor** or **community paediatrician**. If a child is being statutorily assessed, then this same doctor might contribute the formal medical report.

Children with more significant difficulties might already have been referred through to a **Child Development Service** or **hospital paediatrician** or specialist. Parents can tell you who is involved and help you keep in touch with what is happening. Within a Child Development Team, there is usually a range of multidisciplinary professions represented.

Speech and language therapists assess, treat and advise on the needs of children with communication, speech, language and feeding difficulties. They support and work through parents and carers and sometimes work with children individually or in small groups. **Physiotherapists** advise on positioning, movement and balance for young children with motor or physical difficulties. Sometimes they provide direct therapy and often they work through practitioners and parents, advising on mobility aids, seating and positioning, and how to encourage the child to move as independently as possible. **Occupational therapists** aim to make their clients as independent as possible and advise on aids and equipment, developing fine motor skills and developing eye-hand co-ordination.

Often, there is a **clinical psychologist** available to assess and advise on the child's general development and emotional needs. Some of these people work exclusively with children who have behavioural or emotional difficulties. Others have a specialism in child development work and particular disabilities or conditions. Some work in family therapy teams or provide play therapy or art therapy for those children who are struggling to make sense of their lives or feelings.

Social Services

Some children may be known to Social Services and you might find that there is a named **social worker** or **family support worker**. Sometimes, the family support worker works with parents and carers to help them develop the confidence to play with their children and enjoy each other's company in a more positive way. Social Services also play a role in child protection and you may sometimes find yourself asked to contribute to a case review with a team of other professionals.

There may be other professionals or teams involved with SEN in your particular area such as a **SURE START** team or other community-based initiative. Your local Early Years Childcare and Development Partnership should be able to provide you with information about these.

Chapter Eight

Involving the children

Children's opinions and views must be considered valid if we are to include everybody in the educational system in a more democratic and inclusive way. The *SEN Code of Practice* asks us to consider ways in which we can make sure that children are included in their own assessments and planning as far as possible. In this chapter, we explore some of the ways of involving children with SEN in their own assessment and planning of provision at the Foundation Stage.

Holding on to principles

A useful starting point is to be clear about the principles we hold when assessing and working with young children who have special educational needs:

- Assessment should be carried out with a proper respect for the children themselves.

- We must respect their culture, their ethnicity, their language, their religion, their age and their gender.

- The methods we choose for assessment and intervention must be respectful of all children regardless of their gifts, abilities or specific learning needs.

- Care and education of young children are not two separate, discrete activities. As a consequence, when we work with young children, we should attend to their whole development and lives and not to certain aspects of it.

- Early years educators inevitably have power. This needs to be acknowledged and used lovingly, wisely and well.

- The interests of the child should always be paramount. Assessment and intervention must enhance their lives, their learning and their development. It must 'work' for the child.

Involving young children

Schools are encouraged to discuss the purpose of a particular assessment arrangement with a child, invite comments from the child and consider the use of pupil reports and systematic feedback to the child concerned. Many children with special educational needs have little self-confidence and low self-esteem. Involving children in tracking their own progress within a programme designed to meet their particular learning or behavioural difficulty can contribute to an improved self-image and greater self-confidence.

What would involvement of the *very young* child 'look like' in practice? For younger children, we can take steps to stand back and **observe** what the child is doing in clear, objective terms: the level and range of play, the situations that encourage most interest or co-operation, signs of pleasure and distress. With such an observation, it might become possible to interpret what is maintaining a pattern of behaviour or play in a child, and to draw up a hypothesis for what is on the child's own agenda. Sometimes we can observe the way children play with 'models' of their world and interpret how they are thinking about it using **small world play**. We can observe the older brother or sister playing with the dolls, acting out considerable feelings of love, anger or fantasy after the arrival of the new baby. It seems that children can usually keep this behaviour distinct and separate from real life and can use it to deal with strong emotions without developing the behaviour at home.

Children's **drawings**, too, have been used extensively in assessing children's developmental levels, emotional states, records of achievement and personal experiences. They form part of the dialogue we are able to share with them and, therefore, form a springboard for further talking and working together. In a similar way, we can use drawings and illustrations as a stimulus for children's own comments and interpretations. This, too, will give us a glimpse of the way they understand their worlds.

We can use **stories** and **picture books** as a means of introducing situations and encouraging dialogue. Early years settings have built up useful collections of stimulus books for covering a range of new situations the child might meet; going to hospital, having a new baby in the family, living with one parent; why not 'My Statutory Assessment' or 'Ali's Special Needs'? You may find the booklet *Taking Part* (Mortimer, 2000) a useful tool here.

In a similar way **welcome profiles** can be adapted and developed in order to gather information about the child's view on entry into a setting. A welcome profile is a form which parents complete (or an interview which you hold together) gathering information before a child starts in your setting and making parents and child feel welcomed. Open-ended questioning to parents and carers such as 'Tell me about a favourite toy/activity/family outing/memory'; 'Is there anything which makes your child particularly frightened?'; 'How much help does she need when going to the toilet?'; or 'How does he let you know when he is cross/happy/upset?' allows you to gather honest information about all children regardless of special need. These questions do not beg a certain reply and license the parent to describe freely the amount of help that might be needed or to celebrate a new-found independence.

Child-centred assessments

The use of play-based approaches for assessing and helping children makes the whole process child-centred and enjoyable. There will usually be ways in which we can ensure the assessment arises naturally from a familiar situation in which the child is enabled to show of his/her best as well as his/her level of need. This is most likely to happen at home and sometimes we may need to 'lift' our assessment into more than one setting in order to gain the fullest picture of the child.

The *Playladders* checklist (see page 50) was devised to take the process of play-based assessment into a group setting. You can also use your regular play activities to observe and assess how a child is responding to your interventions. Registered early years settings are already used to making opportunities for regular assessment and monitoring in the work they do with all the children.

Including *all* children

Make sure that the teaching materials and books within your early years setting reflect a wide range of ability, ethnicity and culture. Picture books which contain images of differently abled children can act as talking points for diversity and difference. Most libraries have now developed specialist sections of books which relate to a wide range of special educational needs. Some cover certain conditions in the stories they contain. Others will appeal and be helpful to young children at certain stages of exploring and talking, such as 'multi-sensory' or 'interactive' books which can be enjoyed at many levels at once. You will find many ideas and resources in the series *Special Needs in the Early Years* (see page 51).

In order to ensure that *all* children have access to the learning environment, you will need to make certain modifications to the physical structure of the space, the approaches used or the routine followed. This is what it means to be 'inclusive' in your approach. You need to think about the arrangement of furniture and fittings to make sure that they are physically accessible by all the children. You may need to store resources at child-height for the child who cannot yet walk, or use soft furnishings, carpets and curtains to absorb sounds and facilitate floor play for the child with sensory or physical difficulties. Pictures to label storage spaces or photographs to signal coat-hooks enable all children to identify where things go.

Pictures or symbols can be used to help children to express choices or understand what comes next in a sequence of activities if they have communication difficulties. Sometimes you may need to 'sandwich' short structured activities with free play making it easier for the child with attention difficulties to concentrate for longer. You might also need to plan opportunities for a child to think and play in quieter distraction-free areas. Specialist tools can be obtained for making computer equipment accessible to all children. The opportunity to work in large and small groups, and sometimes individually, can again provide opportunities for all children to learn in a variety of situations and ways.

Remember that your greatest tool in meeting needs inclusively is your ability to be flexible and the fact that you are already used to catering for a wide range of ages and stages in the early years. If you can hold on to the philosophy that children are children first and that each child has individual and unique needs, then you are already on the journey towards inclusion.

Appendix – Example policy

Sunnyholme Nursery School
Special Educational Needs Policy

We believe that *all* children have a right to a broad and balanced early years curriculum. Sunnyholme Nursery welcomes all children whatever their individual needs and believes in providing an inclusive setting. In order to achieve this we work closely with parents and carers and, where necessary, other agencies.

We aim to identify any difficulties a child might have and to work with parents and carers to address those difficulties.

Admission

We offer admission to all children living in the .... area of the town aged 2 years 6 months to school age. In certain circumstances, some children may require additional resources of some kind. Parents of children with particular needs should approach the SENCO for more information.

How we support those with special educational needs (SEN)

Our Special Educational Needs Co-ordinator or 'SENCO' is .... and he/she:

- assists in identifying any difficulties a child might have;

- helps plan approaches and strategies;

- keeps parents and carers in touch with progress;

- reviews this SEN policy each year;

- knows about outside agencies who can help;

- acts as a resource for all staff regarding SEN.

Training

The following members of staff have had training in special educational needs:

1. ....
2. ....

Staff attend SEN training regularly through the Early Years Childcare and Development Partnership's Training Forum. Last year, staff attended the following courses:

1. ....
2. ....

Our SENCO attends four days SEN training each year and attends regular cluster meetings to share approaches and ideas. We have a range of books and pamphlets on SEN and support services and these are available for parents and carers to see.

We currently receive weekly input from a visiting speech and language therapist: ....

Some staff are trained in the use of 'Makaton' sign language.

Identifying SEN and taking action

1. With regard to the identification of all children's strengths and weaknesses:

   • We observe the progress that *all* the children make and note any child who seems to be having difficulties in any area of learning. This includes children who are having difficulties in behaving and concentrating.

   • We record progress and share it with parents regularly.

   • If we feel that a child needs something additional to or different from our usual provision, we discuss this with parents and prepare an individual education plan (IEP) outlining clear targets for that child. This is called Early Years Action.

- We review this plan regularly (at least once a month) with parents or carers.

- We plan ways in which parents and carers can also support their child's progress at home.

- At every stage, and wherever practically possible, the child will be involved in the assessment process and his/her views sought.

2. We can request further support through Early Years Action Plus:

- If, with the resources normally available to us, we all feel that a child is still experiencing difficulties and his or her needs are not adequately being met, we can request further support and advice through our named support professionals. This may, for example, involve one or more of the following: early years support teacher; behaviour support teacher; educational psychologist; sensory support teacher; specialist health visitor; speech and language therapist.

- The SENCO will liaise with external professionals in drawing up an IEP and planning suitable strategies.

- The SENCO will organise review meetings with external professionals, parents, carers and the key worker to monitor progress.

3. If the child's needs remain so substantial that they cannot be met effectively within the resources normally available to our setting, the SENCO, after consultation with parents, carers and external professionals, will request the LEA to carry out a statutory assessment. The SENCO will co-ordinate all reports, review meeting notes etc. and submit these to the LEA with the relevant paperwork.

Planning support for children with SEN

We endeavour to provide an inclusive environment by:

- making sure that our long, medium and short-term planning for all the children also contain approaches and activities for ensuring the progress of those children who have SEN;

- differentiating our activities so that they are achievable by all children and that all children experience success and gain confidence;

- adapting our materials and teaching styles to deliver our learning activities to children with different individual needs;

- monitoring how each child with SEN learns, using a key worker system.

We keep parents and carers in touch with their child's progress through termly meetings when their child has SEN. We also put together an 'All About Me' book for you to share with your child, detailing our approaches and activities that term with photographs and records of work. We do not contact another professional about a child without parental consent, unless there are concerns about child protection.

Premises

Our premises are suitable for wheelchair access. We have a discrete nappy changing area and a quiet room for small group work. Our outdoor play area has soft, safety paving.

Monitoring our SEN Policy

We monitor our SEN policy by:

- reviewing it annually (September);

- circulating it to all parents and carers annually;

- asking parents, carers and staff regularly about how well we are meeting SEN in our setting;

- talking with the children about how happy they feel about their setting and their play.

Transition arrangements

We pass our progress reports, plans and assessments on to the next setting or school your child will attend. The SENCO liaises with other settings if a child with SEN attends more than one.

Complaints procedure

Complaints about SEN provision should be made to the SENCO initially. She/he will report back within a week and also provide a next line of contact if the matter has not been resolved to mutual satisfaction.

Signed: ....

Date: ....

References

DfES (2001) *The Special Educational Needs Code of Practice.* Nottingham: DfES Publications.

Dickins, M. and Denziloe, J. (1998) *All Together: How to Create Inclusive Services for Disabled Children and their Families.* London: National Early Years Network.

Qualifications and Curriculum Authority (QCA) (2000) *Curriculum Guidance for the Foundation Stage.* Hayes: QCA Publications.

Sebba, J. and Sachdev, D. (1997) *What Works in Inclusive Education?* Ilford: Barnados.

Useful resources

Birkett, V. (2000) *How to Survive and Succeed as a SENCO in the Primary School.* Cambridge: LDA.

DfES (2001) *The SEN Toolkit.* DfES.

Education Act 1996. London: HMSO.

Mortimer, H. (2000) *Taking Part.* Lichfield: QEd.

Mortimer, H. (2000) *Developing Individual Behaviour Plans in Early Years Settings.* Tamworth: NASEN.

Mortimer, H. (2000) *Playladders.* Lichfield: QEd.

Mortimer, H. (2000) *The Music Makers Approach: Inclusive Activities for Young Children with Special Educational Needs.* Tamworth: NASEN.

Mortimer, H. (2000) *Starting Out: Preparing young children with special educational needs for a new school.* Lichfield: QEd.

Mortimer, H. (2001) *Personal, Social and Emotional Development of Children in the Early Years.* Lichfield: QEd.

Mortimer, H. (2001) *Special Needs and Early Years Provision.* London: Continuum.

Mortimer, H. (2001) *The Observation and Assessment of Children in the Early Years.* Lichfield: QEd.

Mortimer, H. (2002) *Supporting Children with AD/HD and Attention Difficulties.* Lichfield: QEd,

Pre-school Learning Alliance (2002) *The Role of the Special Educational Needs Co-ordinator (SENCO) in Pre-school Settings.* London: Pre-school Learning Alliance.

Special Needs in the Early Years series. Leamington Spa: Scholastic (all by Hannah Mortimer, 2001 – 2002).
Meeting SEN in Early Years (Series handbook).
Helping Children with Autistic Spectrum Difficulties.
Helping Children with Behavioural and Emotional Difficulties.
Helping Children with Learning Difficulties.
Helping Children with Medical Difficulties.
Helping Children with Physical and Co-ordination Difficulties.
Helping Children with Sensory Difficulties.
Helping Children with Speech and Language Difficulties.

Organisations and support groups

The CaF Directory of specific conditions and rare syndromes in children (including those that affect behaviour) with their family support networks can be obtained on subscription from Contact a Family, Equity House, 209–211 City Road, London EC1V 1JN

Department for Education and Skills (DfES), Sanctuary Buildings, Great Smith Street, London SW1P 3BT
Tel: 0870 000 2288   Fax: 01928 794248   Email: info@dfes.gov.uk
Web site: www.dfes.gov.uk

The National Association for Special Educational Needs (NASEN), 4/5 Amber Business Village, Amber Close, Tamworth B77 4RP
Tel: 01827 311500   Fax: 01827 313005   Email: welcome@nasen.org.uk
Web site: www.nasen.org.uk

National Children's Bureau (NCB), 8 Wakley Street, London EC1V 1NG
Tel: 020 7843 6000   Fax: 020 7278 9512
Web site: www.ncb.org.uk

National Early Years Network (for customised in-house training), 77 Holloway Road, London N7 8JZ
Tel: 020 7607 9573   Fax: 020 7700 1105

Pre-school Learning Alliance, 69 Kings Cross Road, London WC1X 9LL
Tel: 020 7833 0991   Fax: 020 7837 4942
Web site: www.pre-school.org.uk

Qualifications and Curriculum Authority (QCA), 83 Piccadilly, London W1J 8QA
Tel: 020 7509 5555   Fax: 020 7509 6666
Web site: www.qca.org.uk

QEd Publications, The Rom Building, Eastern Avenue, Lichfield, Staffs. WS13 6RN
Tel: 01543 416353   Fax: 01543 419144   Email: orders@qed.uk.com
Web site: www.qed.uk.com

Save the Children *Working with Under Eights* (leaflets, books and training on a wide range of issues including SEN) 17 Grove Lane, London SE5 8RD